The Takoradi Run

Bob Kerr

In with a chance

Wellington, 1926

I was flying. And when I landed on the mat I knew I was in with a chance. My parents were pleased. Mum took me to a studio down town and had this photograph taken, and she had my name engraved on the cup: Ron Witcombe. Winner. YMCA Gymnastics Cup. 1926.

She put the photo next to the telephone on top of the china cabinet in the front room.

The front room was only for visitors. The curtains were kept closed so the light wouldn't fade the furniture.

She wasn't my real mum.

My real mum used to take me and my sister Win on the tram to Island Bay. She would spread

a big red rug out on the sand and watch Win and me swimming and building castles and turning over rocks to watch the crabs scuttle away. Then we'd have a Frosty Jack ice cream before we got the tram home.

Then again, maybe I've made that up. Tricky thing, memory — it doesn't always tell you the truth.

When our mum started spending days in bed, we weren't told why.

'Don't trouble the children,' the grown-ups whispered in the hall. One day she went away in an ambulance. We didn't visit her in hospital.

'They won't understand.' the grown-ups said.

Dad was doing up his tie one morning when the telephone rang. It was the hospital.

We didn't go to her funeral.

'It will just upset them,' they said.

She died of a kidney infection. A kidney infection that penicillin would have fixed in no time at all, but there was no penicillin then. The first time I heard about penicillin was during the war in Cairo. We needed it then. But I'll get to that later.

My sister Win was a couple of years older than me. She went all quiet after Mum died, wouldn't say boo to a goose — didn't trust anyone. Me, I'd climb up on anyone's knee. I was everyone's friend, but I didn't trust anyone either.

I've got one photograph of my real mum, it's blurry and out of focus. She is on the Wellington south coast with a bicycle. I don't know who the taller woman in the photo is. Was it a friend? Was it her sister?

On Sunday mornings I'd be dressed in a freshly ironed white shirt and Win would wear her white frock with the embroidered flowers and we would walk along Grafton Road to Sunday School. Miss Jenkins would play the piano and we would sing, 'There is a Green Hill far away without a city wall, where our dear lord was crucified — he died to save us all.'

God didn't save our mother. If he'd remembered, she would have been there, waiting for us after school.

Above Miss Jenkins' piano there was a picture showing a wide road lined with brightly lit shops, cinemas and hotels with flash cars parked outside. Over the hills next to the town was a narrow, rocky path. A pilgrim was making his way along this path with a huge burden on his back. Miss Jenkins insisted we were better off taking the rocky road. The shops and the cinemas and the flash cars were what Miss Jenkins called 'temptations to be avoided'. It didn't make sense to me. Why didn't the pilgrim just catch a cab and go to the movies?

Perhaps the green hill far away was the Karori Cemetery. After Sunday School we'd catch the tram there. Dad would sit on the edge of the concrete grave for hours. If Win and I ran around and made too much noise, he would growl.

A year later he married Anne Duncan, the housekeeper. Anne Duncan wore a dead fox around her shoulders. A fox fur stole — is that what it's called? It had a snout and little dangly legs and beady, brown glass eyes.

We stopped visiting the cemetery and moved to the new house opposite Hataitai School.

Our real mum was never mentioned again. At school we had to pretend that Anne Duncan was our real mum.

We had clean hankies and neatly folded clothes. On Mondays we had cold roast mutton, but our world was like the front room. Dark, cold and silent.

Just follow the instructions

Wellington, 1928

I didn't understand the plans for the P class dinghy. Win had to explain.

'It's like a dress pattern,' she said. 'They give you the correct shape to cut out.'

Win made all her own clothes on the treadle sewing machine. When she finished making a dress, she would get me to take a photo of her wearing it.

Because Win was a snappy dresser she was often photographed by street photographers when we went to town.

I started building the P class in the basement. I could hear Win upstairs whirring away on the Singer.

First you built the frame, and then you turned it upside down and put the planks on. Win and I would run up and down the stairs with the kettle to steam the planks so they would bend. You had to leave a gap of three eighths of an inch and caulk it. When you put

it in the water, the planks would swell, which made it watertight.

I gave the tiller, the mast and the deck three coats of varnish — it was looking pretty flash. But it was too wide to fit through the door. I had to take the door frame off to get it out. The old man wasn't happy.

My mate Ben Crosby also built a P class. Ben and I went through school together and played rugby on Saturday mornings. Ben built his P class in his dad's garage. His dad had to leave their Morrie out on the street. Ben's dad was good like that.

DAD HELPED ME BUY THE TIMBER, FITTINGS AND THE SAILS FOR THE P CLASS. WE GOT IT DOWN TO EVANS BAY ON THE RUNNING BOARD OF THE CAR.

...AND IT WOULD NOSE-DIVE RUNNING DOWNWIND.
I THOUGHT IT WAS FANTASTIC!

Our first jaunt was across Evans Bay, around the point of the Miramar Peninsula.

Out in the middle of the bay there were different birds. I was used to the shore birds. The red-billed gulls that would huddle in the middle of the beach, all facing into the wind; the gulls on the outside keeping watch while those in the centre would tuck their heads under their wings and sleep. A few yards away, solitary black-billed gulls and oystercatchers would strut about, pecking at the kelp left by the last tide.

Out in the middle of the bay there were little blue penguins that you could get close to before they disappeared under the water. Flutters of shearwaters and terns diving for tiny fish.

From the end of the peninsula we could see Ward Island.

'We could camp there,' said Ben.

The next weekend there was a gentle southerly. We made a run for it. It was the first time I'd been away from home.

Ben told his folks where we were going. I didn't. When we got back on Sunday afternoon, the old man was furious.

Breakfast, dinner and a cut lunch

Wellington, 1929

On Friday nights, people would come to Dad's shop, Witcombe and Caldwell — gunmakers, fishing tackle and sports equipment dealers. They would get themselves kitted out for the weekend with fishing rods, small bore rifles, tents, tennis racquets, golfclubs and rugby balls. On Monday they'd be back in the shop getting their racquets restrung and their fishing rods re-whipped and rubber patches on their waders.

We could afford holidays to Rotorua. Winding our way out of town over the Paekākāriki hill. Me and Win in the backseat. The first night we would stay in the Tokaanu Hotel. Early in the morning the old man would go fishing with all that kit that fly fishermen love. Wet and dry flies in their books and boxes, folding landing nets and pliers for yanking the hook out of the fish's mouth. I didn't like the taste of trout — all those tiny bones stuck in your teeth.

After Tokaanu it would be on to Rotorua. The last time we went, it would have been in 1929, we had our photograph taken with the penny divers. The penny divers didn't look all that happy. They must have had the same photo taken countless times by the same bored photographer. They had stopped smiling for the camera long before we lined up on the far side of their pool. That's me in the striped blazer on the right hand side of the photo. Win whizzed the blazer up on the sewing machine. Pretty flash, I thought. Dad and Anne Duncan are over on the left.

Silence followed. The clock above the fireplace ticked, the minute hand nudged forward, sixty ticks and it was back where it started. Knives and forks clattered on the dinner plates. Above the clock, a mirror reflected the back of the old man's head. His hair was turning grey. I looked at the silver beet and potatoes on my plate.

'One tennis ball,' he repeated. 'You have to get a job.'

I was dead keen to get a job. I had applied for over forty jobs and hadn't got a single reply. I wanted out, out of college, out of going on holiday with my parents, out of the house and out of town. To do that I had to have a job. There weren't any jobs. None. I was stuck at home in my school shorts.

Win had a job. She worked in the typing pool at the Education Department and played mixed doubles at the Hataitai Tennis Club on the weekend. She gave most of her wages to Dad and Anne Duncan for board. Even the penny divers had an income. Grasping pennies from the mud at the bottom of their pool.

On the Monday after the tennis ball announcement there was an ad in the *Evening Post* for an office boy. It said, 'Send an application to Box 198, Wellington.' In those days, employers would put a box number in their ads because they didn't want a long line of unemployed people queueing down the footpath. Next morning, I jumped on my bike, pedalled to the Post Office and found Box 198. I waited all morning. Office juniors in drab frocks came and emptied boxes. Secretaries in high heeled shoes came, business men in grey suits came. For half an hour, nobody came to the box I was interested in. In the early afternoon a bloke in a brown jacket arrived and turned the key to Box 198. He emptied all the job applications into a large flagon bag. He picked out an envelope that looked different from all the others and opened it. I peered over his shoulder. It was a bill addressed to Brown and Dureau, Importers Agents, Brandon Street. I was out the door and back on my bike. When the guy in the brown jacket arrived back at Brown and Dureau, I was waiting.

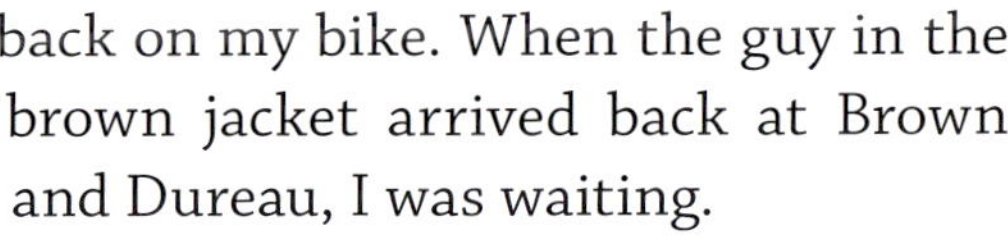

'I've come for the job,' I said.

He looked at me.

'You were the boy at the Post Office.'

'Yep.'

My first task was to throw out all the other applications.

Next Saturday, Ben came around to collect me for rugby. I had my bag packed ready. I never came back.

I got a nice set-up with a widow with a spare room in Newtown. I earned three pounds a week. I paid my landlady 25 shillings a week for breakfast, dinner and a cut lunch.

After a year Ben and I sold our P class dinghies and bought a fourteen-footer. It needed painting. It needed new sails. It needed everything. We set to work.

If it tipped over, you couldn't stand on the centreboard and pull it up again like the P class. You had to wait for a tow, and when the tow arrived, it was often to the nearest beach.

I was sixteen. The youngest skipper in Wellington. Saturday was racing day: we'd do one race with the Evans Bay Club and then tack around Point Jerningham into the inner harbour and race with the Port Nicholson Club. Then we'd go over to Days Bay. The keelers would come in with a keg of beer and there would be all sorts of drunken races. I stored my sails with a club member up in Rata Road. He had an Idle-Along and I helped him paint it. He gave me a bottle of wine. I drank the whole thing and spent the night sitting on the end of the Patent Slip jetty, spewing my guts into the harbour.

Flying a spelling mistake

Wellington, 1938

Ben's dad was a schoolteacher. His house was up on Mt Victoria. It was full of books. There weren't books in our house. Anne Duncan reckoned they wore out your eyes. When Ben finished school, he went up to the University and studied what he called the classics — the Greeks, the Romans, and the ancient Egyptians. I wasn't brainy like that. I went to night school at the Tech and studied maths and office management.

After he graduated, Ben landed a flash scholarship to Oxford University in England. I was proud of him, so were his mum and dad. We all went down to the boat to see him off.

'Look after the fourteen-footer,' he said, shaking my hand.

As we walked back to the tram, his mum said, 'I hope that Mr Hitler doesn't start a war'.

A year later I got a letter from Ben.

It's cold here, the sun rises in the middle of the morning and sets in the middle of the afternoon. Mr Hitler has taken over a bit of Czechoslovakia and invaded Poland. The Royal Navy has mistaken my ability to sail a P class dinghy for nautical competence, so now I'm Sub-lieutenant Crosby on Her Majesty's Destroyer, Fearless. *I'll get back to the Egyptians and the Greeks next year when the wee corporal has been sorted.*

I know you won't get around to writing. But that's OK. We'll catch up sooner or later.

I kept the job at Brown and Dureau right through the slump. I asked the boss if I could get a raise on account of the night classes. He just laughed.

Ads appeared in *The Evening Post* saying that duty called the youth of New Zealand to join the Air Force. I didn't give two hoots about duty; it was the passage to England borne by the state that interested me.

To join the Air Force, you had to have School Certificate. I didn't, but I noticed the words 'or equivalent standard'. I went to the Tech and asked to see my night school record. It wasn't very good but the headmaster thought I was very patriotic and he wrote a letter saying that my night classes were the equivalent of School Certificate.

Bingo! I was in the Air Force!

Win turned up the trousers and tucked in the jacket. I went to the studio where I had the photograph taken with the Gymnastics Cup and had another snap taken. Maybe it ended up on top of the china cabinet. Maybe it didn't. I never went back to find out.

We did our ground training at Weraroa. We lived in tents and didn't have to wash dishes or peel potatoes. Instead, it was gunnery, aerial photography and bomb aiming.

I was worried that the Brits might make peace with Hitler before I arrived, so instead of training to be a pilot I did navigation. It was a shorter course.

In our first class, the instructor unrolled a big aerial photo and said 'Where is this? Which way is north? What day is it? What's the time and which way is the wind blowing?'

Ray Dudunski pointed to a square in the middle of the town. 'See, there, the railway runs through the middle of the square.' It was Palmerston North. Arkwright reckoned that the sun was shining, but there were no long shadows, which meant it would be the middle of the day, and what shadows were there must have been pointing south.

We were stumped on the day.

'Look closely,' said the instructor. 'There's washing on the clothes lines, it's probably Monday and the washing is all blowing in the same direction, so that tells you the wind is from the west.'

We shifted up the road to the air base at Ohakea for our flight training. At Ohakea there was a huge new concrete hanger. There were new runways, new offices, a new control tower, new cups and saucers in the mess, new soap in the showers and very old aircraft.

WE'RE GOING TO LEARN TO FLY IN A SPELLING MISTAKE?

NZ 102

A SLOW, OBSOLETE SPELLING MISTAKE.

We plotted courses along the Taranaki coast, in our out-of-date, biplanes searching for imaginary submarines. Then we blasted them out of the water with our imaginary torpedoes.

I thought it was fantastic, like the first time I put the P class in the water, but this time it wasn't water, it was air. I was flying.

Win took this photo of me in my flying kit on the day of the passing out parade.

No more stumbling to the tram every morning for another dreary day at Brown and Dureau. I was out of there with the passage to England borne by the state, just like it said in the ad.

We sailed on the *Akaroa*. The old man, Anne Duncan and Win came down to Aotea Quay to see me off.

'I'm on my own now,' Win whispered.

'You'll be fine,' I said.

'Write to me, send something so I know where you are.'

I walked up the gangplank with Dudunski and Arky. I didn't look back.

Empty chairs

RAF (Royal Air Force) Whatton, Norfolk, England, August 1940

We were assigned to 82 squadron, based at Watton, in the middle of the flat Norfolk countryside. It wasn't those flash Harrys in their spitfires with their natty little moustaches that won the Battle of Britain. It was us: Arkwright, Dudunski and me. We bombed the invasion barges. Hitler couldn't get enough of them together in the channel ports.

We'd do two bombing runs a day. One in the morning, back to Watton for lunch, and then another in the afternoon.

We were returning from one run over the channel ports when a blast of cannon fire from a German fighter ripped through the cockpit.

'Where did he come from?' yelled Dudunski from the gun turret. 'Are you guys still there?'

I checked — two arms, two legs, no blood.

Arky flung the Blenheim into the bank of cloud. 'I'm still in one piece,' he called. There were neat round holes in the Perspex windows. The engines were still whirring, we weren't leaking gas, nothing was on fire, but the big compass on the instrument panel, just to the left of Arky's knees, was a mess of mangled metal and shattered glass.

We ploughed on through the cloud that hid us from the German fighter and obscured the landscape below.

‘I have no idea where we’re headed,’ said Arky. ‘The compass is kaput.’ I reached into the pocket of my flight jacket. There was the compass Dad had given me for the P class. I flicked open the brass lid, looked at our last position on the map, gave Arky a bearing and handed him the compass. It led us all the way home to Whatton.

After the barges, it was daylight bombing over Germany. On our first trip, we came out of the cloud crossing the Dutch border. Below in the morning sun were brown ploughed fields and dark green woods surrounded by lighter green that followed the contours of the hills. Were those grapes? I wondered, as we inched forward. Villages with churches, and houses with white walls and red tile roofs, were tucked in the valleys. There were only three or four fields between some of the villages. There was washing on the lines like the photograph our instructor showed us on our first day at Wereroa. A railway wound its way around the hills through stations with rows of wagons in sidings, past quarries and factories with smoke stacks. In front of us, exactly where it should be, was the Rhine. Barges like the ones we bombed in the Channel ports were making their way along the river.

Black bursts of flack popped around the Blenheim. Arky started weaving. There was a close explosion, a sound like gravel being thrown at a tin shed. The Blenheim shuddered.

‘How long to go?’ asked Arky. I looked at my watch. ‘Twenty-five minutes.’

‘Where is the cloud when you need it?’

Daylight bombing changed to night-time bombing. I preferred the night runs. It was harder to work out exactly where we were, but after a while I recognised the configurations of searchlights around German cities like Essen and Hamburg. They were visible from fifty miles away. The night fighters didn’t follow us through the bursting flack as we came in over the target and I was too busy making sure we are in the right place to worry.

YOU COULD LIGHT YOUR SMOKE OFF THAT BEAM.
THREE MINUTES TO GO.

READY WHEN YOU ARE. STEADY... STEADY...

They'd send out aircraft the next day to take photographs to see what we'd hit. We weren't very successful. We dropped bombs in lakes and peppered empty paddocks with craters. If the weather was crook and I got a bearing wrong, or I didn't get the wind speed right, we could end up flying out into the North Sea until we ran out of gas. My mate Murphy clipped a line of trees past the end of the runway and cartwheeled into a barn. Like the Vildebeest, the Blenheim was now obsolete. It had been replaced by aircraft that could fly higher, further and faster. Blenheims were shot down by the dozen.

At breakfast there would be empty chairs. I learnt not to ask. I learnt to be everybody's friend and not to get too attached to anyone.

I don't know why I lived and others didn't.

After our thirty-trip tour of duty, Dudunski, Arky and I were re-assigned.

No bombs, no blackouts, no ration books

Takoradi, 1941

WE TRAVELLED TO TAKORADI BY SHIP.

WHY AFRICA?

PETROL. MR. ROMMEL IS A BIT SHORT OF PETROL.

Field Marshal Rommel's Afrika Korps were racing along the top of Africa, planning to capture Cairo and the Arabian oil fields. If we flew enough planes across the desert to Cairo, we would be able to stop him and change the course of the war. That was the plan anyway.

But first, our planes had to be unloaded from the ship, trucked to the big factory at the airport and assembled. We had to wait.

Takoradi was a great place to wait: no bombs, no blackouts, no ration books.

Sun, beaches, palm trees, fishing. A British colony, just like New Zealand.

Mosquitoes . . . there were a few mosquitoes.

'You'll need a mosquito net.'

'Where do we get that?'

'Ask Kwame.'

'Tropical kit?'

'Kwame will sort that out.'

'Where's Kwame?'

'Stores.'

Kwame did sort us out. He also suggested that I give him a hand loading his truck. We drove down the coast to the town of Axim and loaded the truck with fresh fish, tomatoes, cabbages, bananas and pineapples. You couldn't get bananas in England and I'd never eaten a pineapple.

There was a castle in Axim, like an old English castle.

'Fort Saint Anthony,' said Kwame. 'It was built by the Portuguese, taken over by the Dutch and then the British.'

We drove up to the castle, but there was no one around. We crossed an inner courtyard and walked through an arched doorway into the dark.

I CAN'T SEE A THING. WHERE ARE WE?

YOU'RE IN A SLAVE DUNGEON. THIS IS A SLAVE CASTLE.

'Slaves were imprisoned here before they were loaded onto ships to cross the Atlantic for America.'

I stuffed my tobacco back in my pocket and hurried out into the light. We climbed up onto the castle battlements and looked out over the Atlantic Ocean.

Halfway back to Takoradi, Kwame turned down a dirt road.

'Couple of things to drop off,' he said. It started to rain. The wiper squeaked back and forth, it couldn't keep up with the downpour. Kwame weaved the truck through the scrub at the edge of the road to avoid potholes. Three men on a motorbike careered towards us out of the rain. They charged straight through the potholes, laughing, sending mud flying. We pulled over to let them past.

'I know those guys,' said Kwame. 'They're crazy.'

The road ended at a ragged group of corrugated iron sheds at the edge of a steep ravine. We ran to the nearest shed. Our shirts were soaked and our shoes covered with mud. Through the trees I could hear heavy machinery thumping. Kwame talked in Fanti to some men who were

carefully pouring a slurry of mud through sluice boxes. The men looked at me, then nodded to Kwame. We walked over to the edge of the ravine and looked down at a swirling river of yellow earth. There was a line of small tin sheds. Mud-covered men were carrying baskets of rocks on their heads up the side of the ravine, their feet slipping and skidding in the soil.

'The sheds follow the gold seam,' said Kwame. 'Under each one there's a shaft, and each shaft is worked by one gang.'

'This is a gold mine?'

'Yes, I worked here before I became a store-keeper for your Air Force.'

We ducked back into the big shed and watched the men running the muddy mixture through the sluice boxes.

'Where's the gold?' I asked.

'It gets trapped on the blanket in the bottom of the box. Then this guy here, he amalgamates the gold caught in the blanket with mercury.'

The man opened his palm and showed me a lump of gold.

'It will be fired to burn off the mercury', said Kwame. 'Leaving pure gold.'

The rain had stopped. The miners picked up their empty baskets and climbed back down into the ravine. Kwame and I walked back to the truck. He took two cases of tomatoes and a box of bananas out of the back of the truck and left them by the generator.

On the outskirts of Takoradi, Kwame stopped to fill up the truck. I wandered along the road, past women with baskets of bananas on their heads, past women selling cabbages and pineapples. Past small shops selling purple suits and bright yellow dresses.

'Sir, for you a special price,' a woman called. She held an orange bead neckless. I remembered Win saying, 'Send me something, so I know where you are.' I offered a handful of notes to the shopkeeper. Kwame appeared.

'For my sister,' I said. Kwame took my fistful of money and talked to the woman in Fanti. The woman laughed. Kwame laughed.

'Yes, you pay foreigners' prices,' he said, 'but not those foreigners' prices; my foreigners' prices.' Kwame handed over less than I was going to. The woman gave me the necklace. We got back in the truck.

As we drove into Takoradi, I asked Kwame why he was working for the Air Force and not in the gold mine.

'We've all got to make a quid,' he said.

'Ah, like the penny divers.'

'The penny divers?' asked Kwame.

'Yeah penny divers, they dive for pennies that rich . . . ah, never mind.'

Kwame gestured towards the workers as we drove away. 'See the guy squeezing the mercury out of the gold with his bare hands? In two years' time he'll be funny in the head. If the shaft collapses and you're down there, you're buried. If the pumps stop, you can drown. The mercury and the arsenic and the cyanide go straight into the river. There are children downstream born without arms or legs. The police arrive with guns and shut the operation down. It's their job to keep the gold for your big British gold corporations. Now I'm a store keeper for your Air Force. It doesn't pay as well as gold mining, Mr Witcombe. But it's safer.'

Mother hen and her six chicks

Takoradi, 1941

The planes were finally assembled. We took them up on test flights. Now we were ready to go. It would take five days to get to Cairo. It was the old team: Dudunski, Arkwright and me. Arky in the pilot's seat. Dudunski in the gun turret and on the wireless; and I'm the navigator — just like back in Watton, but this time there were no bombs to aim and no fighters for Dudunski to shoot at. All we had to do was get our Blenheim and the six Hurricane fighters following us from Takoradi across the Sahara Desert to Cairo. Mother hen with her six chicks.

Flying the Hurricanes we had an Australian, a Pole, who always wore a red scarf, three Brits and one Canadian. We couldn't talk to them — the hurricanes didn't have radios; only the Blenheim had a radio. Everyone depended on me to navigate our way to the next landing strip.

We taxied to the end of the runway and turned into the wind. The rumble and bump of the undercarriage on the grass turned to a rattle and roar as we accelerated down the strip. The rear wheel lifted off and the plane levelled up. I watched its shadow race across the ground beneath us, gradually shifting out of focus as we gained height.

There was a family weeding watermelon vines not far from the end of the runway. They stopped to watch, just like the grandads who lent on their spades and looked up from their allotments as we took off from Watton to bomb the invasion barges.

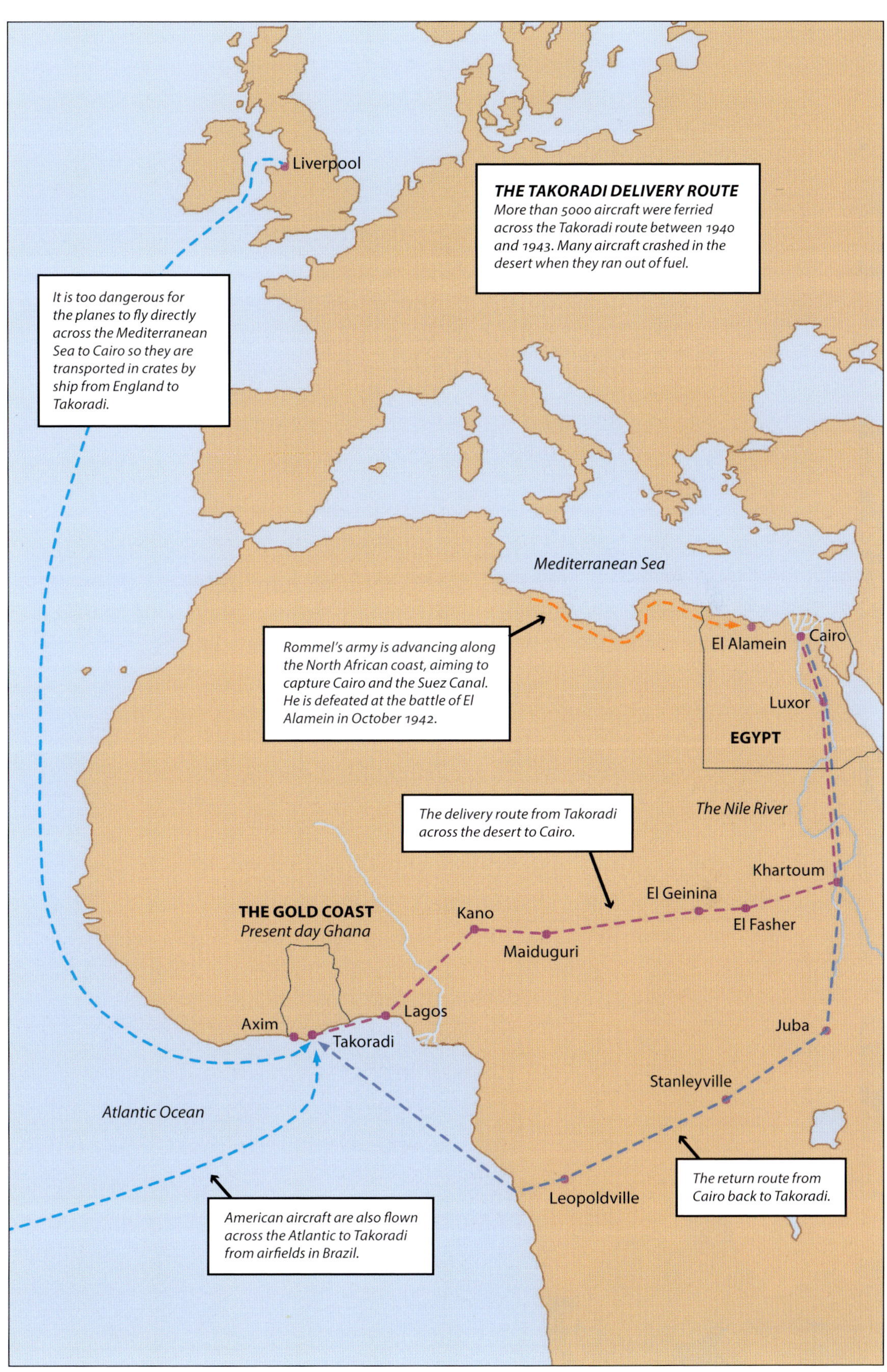
Liverpool
THE TAKORADI DELIVERY ROUTE
More than 5000 aircraft were ferried across the Takoradi route between 1940 and 1943. Many aircraft crashed in the desert when they ran out of fuel.
It is too dangerous for the planes to fly directly across the Mediterranean Sea to Cairo so they are transported in crates by ship from England to Takoradi.
Mediterranean Sea
Rommel's army is advancing along the North African coast, aiming to capture Cairo and the Suez Canal. He is defeated at the battle of El Alamein in October 1942.
El Alamein
Cairo
Luxor
EGYPT
The Nile River
The delivery route from Takoradi across the desert to Cairo.
Khartoum
El Geinina
El Fasher
Kano
Maiduguri
THE GOLD COAST
Present day Ghana
Lagos
Axim
Takoradi
Juba
Stanleyville
Atlantic Ocean
Leopoldville
The return route from Cairo back to Takoradi.
American aircraft are also flown across the Atlantic to Takoradi from airfields in Brazil.

We crossed the coast and banked to the left. I looked down at the port. A ship loaded with more aircraft in crates was sailing in past the breakwater. We circled on around and I saw the Hurricanes taking off. They formed up behind and we headed east down the long beach towards Lagos. The wind from the Atlantic was crashing white surf into the beach and piling clouds against the land. Through gaps in the cloud, I watched the roofs of fishing villages and the Cape Coast slave castle disappear behind us.

The next morning, we headed northeast across the Lagos Lagoon, then over jungle to Oshogbo. Here we altered course by eight degrees to Minna. From Minna it was ninety-four miles to Kaduna. From Kaduna we followed the railway across the Challawa River to the flat-roofed, mud-walled city of Kano.

That evening we had time to look around the city.

IT'S NOT LAMBTON QUAY.

It wasn't a tea shop. It sold gold: gold rings, gold bracelets, gold necklaces. The whole street was full of gold traders. We didn't have a common language between us, but it was clear the shopkeeper thought I should buy a gold ring. I reached into my pocket and pulled out the few notes I had. It wasn't enough for two beers, let alone a gold ring.

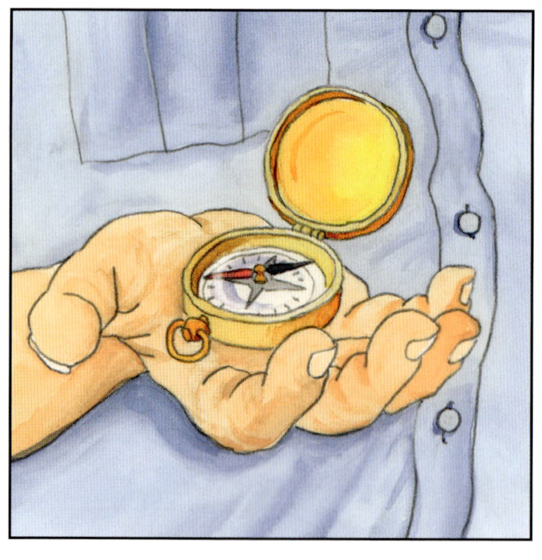

In my pocket I also had the brass compass the old man had given me back in Wellington. The compass Ben and I had used on the fourteen-footer. The compass that got us back to Watton in the cloud when the Blenheim's big compass had been smashed. I took it out.

The gold seller felt its weight, he watched the needle swing around and settle on north. He put the compass in his pocket, picked out the smallest of the rings and gave it to me.

Back at the air strip, I studied the map for the following day's flight. It showed a road all the way to our refuelling stop at Madiguri. After that, there was only empty white paper with no useful landmarks for six hundred and eighty-nine miles to the next stop at El Geneina. Six hundred and eighty-nine miles is about as far as a Hurricane can fly on one tank of gas.

I kept the road in view on the starboard side all morning. After topping up at Madiguri, we flew on into the emptiness.

One good thing about the Blenheim is the greenhouse, the big Perspex windows in the nose. When we'd knocked off our six hundred and eighty-nine miles, I scanned the desert from the greenhouse. We circled the Blenheim searching for El Geneina. It wasn't there.

One of the Hurricanes pulled up alongside. It was the Australian. He indicated that he was out of fuel. The desert below was a sea of sand and dry watercourses. Rocky outcrops poked up through the brown sand. The Hurricane peeled away. We watched it glide down. The pilot knew his wheels would sink in soft sand and flip the plane over so he didn't lower the undercarriage. He flopped it down on its belly. It careered along the sand. The propeller blades bent backwards as they thrashed the ground. It slewed to a halt. Miraculously he had dodged the rocks. The cloud of dust settled. The cockpit canopy slid back and the pilot stepped out.

Our first trip and mother hen had lost one chicken.

We turned the Blenheim and flew on into the brown haze.

Did I get a bearing wrong? Did I get the distance wrong? Did I get the wind speed wrong? I knew the pilots in the five remaining Hurricanes would all be looking at their blinking fuel-warning lights. They were depending on me and I didn't have a clue.

Then, dead ahead, I spied a landing strip with a tin shed, a limp windsock and a pile of fuel cans. A Bedford truck was parked in the shade of the tin shed. On the port side I saw a village of mud brick houses. Everything was disguised in a layer of brown sand.

As we taxied up to the pile of fuel cans, one of the Hurricanes' engines spluttered and cut out. We climbed down onto the sand. A chap with desert shorts down to his knees came out of the tin shed and looked at us standing in the hot sun in our flying kit.

'I was expecting six,' he said.

'We lost one,' said Arky. 'A few minutes back.'

'We should be able to find him in the Bedford,' said desert shorts. 'Let's get you guys refuelled.'

The next day there were mountains between El Geneina and El Fashir with thermal air currents that bounced us around. We could see where to land from miles away.

We climbed out, but this time there was no one to meet us. On the far side of the strip there was a building with a veranda and an open door. We were halfway towards it when Dudunski stopped.

'What's up?' I asked. He pointed. There was a lion standing in the open door. The lion ambled along the veranda, jumped down to the ground and started towards us.

'Back to the Blenheim,' said Arky quietly. 'Don't run.'

We ran like mad.

Behind us we heard, 'Come here, Leo.'

We looked back. There was a bunch of jokers on the veranda laughing. The lion was padding happily back to them.

'Welcome to El Fashir,' they called. 'Leo's alright, he's a pussycat really. We've raised him since he was a cub.

That evening I sat on the veranda. Leo came out and rubbed his chin on my shoulder. He was not the sort of pussycat I would ever get used to.

OUR INSTRUCTIONS THE NEXT MORNING WERE TO: HEAD EAST AND WHEN YOU REACH THE NILE TURN LEFT. KHARTOUM IS AT THE JUNCTION OF THE WHITE NILE AND THE BLUE NILE...

I saw the pyramids before I saw the city. They were huge, pointing heavenward through the haze. We veered over to have a closer look. If Ben was here he would no doubt give me the whole lecture with Cleopatra and Tutankhamun and all that history stuff in the right order.

Dudunski was on the radio, clearing our descent to the airfield at Abu Sueir.

WHAT NOW FOR YOU GUYS?
A COUPLE OF DAYS OFF WHILE THEY RECONDITION THE HURRIES.
THEN WE ASSIST ROMMEL, REARRANGE HIS FRONT LINE.
AND YOU?
WE CATCH THE FLYING BOAT BACK DOWN THE NILE...
...HOP OVER TO THE CONGO RIVER, FLY DOWN TO THE COAST...
...AND GET A SHIP BACK TO TAKORADI.

There were no seats available on the flying boat. Once again we had to wait.

On my first day in Cairo I went to the Egyptian Museum. I knew Ben would ask when I caught up with him, so I thought I'd better have a look. I've still got the map they gave us. You can see the museum there next to the river. Across the river is the island where we got ourselves set up in the hotel — I'll get to that shortly.

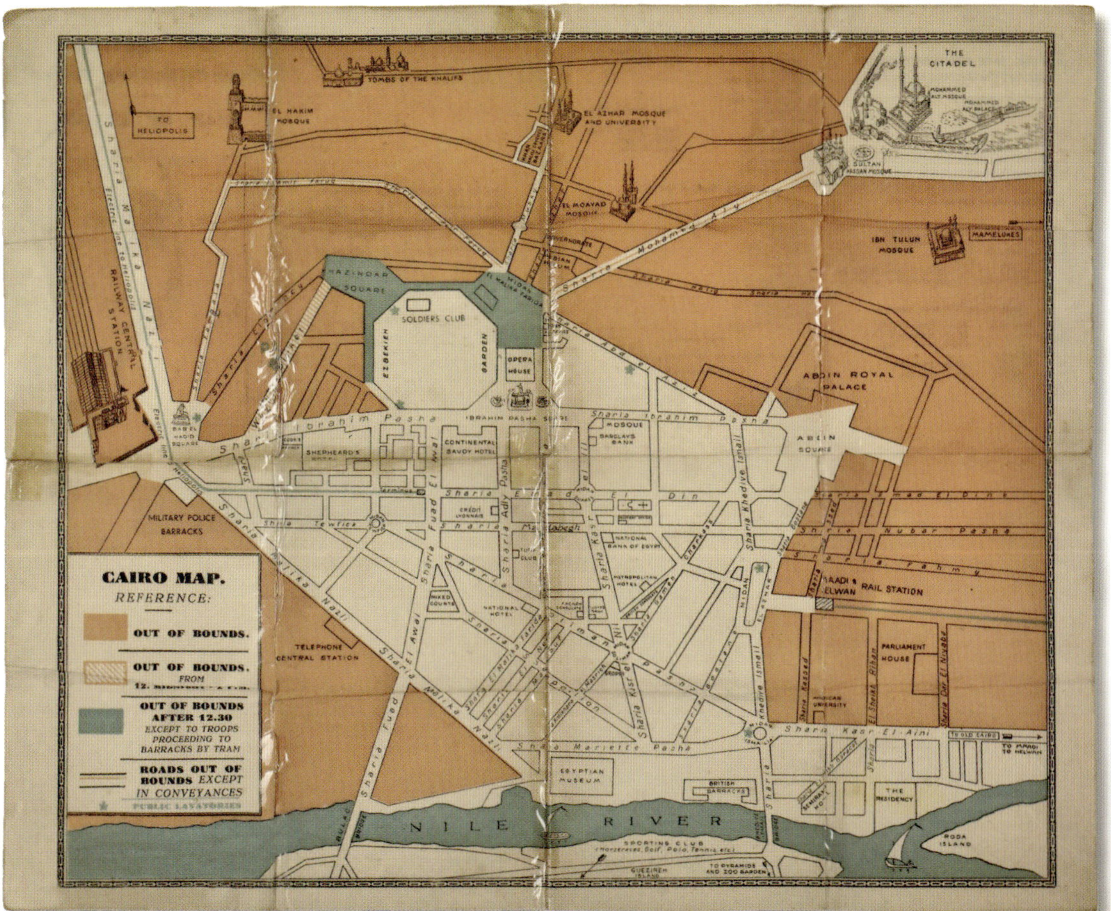

The museum was full of dead Egyptians. I don't know, I got a bit frustrated actually. All those toffs trying to get to heaven, stuffing their burial chambers with golden chariots and chairs and spare sandals and clean shirts they may need in the afterlife. What about the cooks and carpenters and stone masons who built all those tombs? Sorry, you're not rich enough, God isn't going to save you, just like he didn't save our mum.

I could see the builders were pretty smart. They had levels and squares and plum-bobs and scissors and nails and chisels, just like the tools Ben and I used to build our P class dinghies. That's what I'd talk to Ben about.

Finance can be arranged

Cairo, December 1941

On my second day in Cairo I went on a long walk across the crowded city. It was hot and I was pestered by punters trying to sell me things I couldn't afford. A ride in a carriage, freshly baked bread, a fly whisk, a cold drink . . . boy, I could have done with a cold beer.

The American pilots had cash to flash around, but not us. A navigator's wage kept me stuck in barracks with few options for entertainment. It was like being back in Wellington at Brown and Dureau. I was determined not to go back there, but exactly what was I going to do when this war was over? I wasn't sure. What did flying bombers qualify me for anyway?

A FLY WHISK, SIR?
SIR, I DON'T KNOW WHAT YOU WANT, BUT I HAVE IT.
GOLD and SILVER

One street was full of jewellery shops. I could see from the signs in the shop windows that the price of gold was four times what it was in Kano. I did some quick calculations and pushed open the door of one of the shops. There were gold necklaces displayed on purple velvet, trays of gold rings in glass cabinets and a large framed photo of Winston Churchill on the counter. At least I'd chosen a shop on the right side. It was sometimes hard to tell who the Egyptians supported in this war.

SIR, A GLASS OF TEA?
THAT'S A VERY PATRIOTIC PHOTO.

I HAVE LOTS OF TOMMIES FOR CUSTOMERS...

MAYBE SOON I'LL HAVE LOTS OF GERMAN CUSTOMERS.
WE'RE FLEXIBLE, IT'S NOT OUR WAR.

FLIP!
ON THE OTHER SIDE I HAVE THIS GENTLEMAN.

KING FAROUK IS MORE INCLINED THIS WAY.

DING! DING!

FLIP!
GOOD AFTERNOON, MADAM.

Two Brits in uniform entered the shop. Mr Fish (that's what I came to call the shopkeeper, Charlie Fish, on account of the fish he had embroidered on the lapel of his jacket) quickly flipped the photograph back to Winston Churchill. He opened the glass cabinet behind the counter and took out a tray of gold rings. 'This would suit you,' he said offering one to the woman. She tried it on her finger.

'How does that fit?' he asked.

The woman smiled.

'Finance can be arranged.'

After the couple left, Mr Fish asked me what I did. I told him about flying planes across the Sahara for the Desert Air Force.

'Empty planes?'

'How much are the rings?'

'It depends on the quality of the gold,' said Mr Fish.

'Are you interested in this?' I asked, pointing to my gold ring.

'Didn't it last?'

'I didn't want it in the first place.'

Mr Fish eased the ring off my finger and bit it.

'That's quality,' he said. 'Where did you get it?'

I told him about visiting the mine with Kwame and the gold market in Kano.

'Could you bring me more?' asked Mr Fish. 'Finance can be arranged. Meet me on the terrace of Shepherds Hotel tomorrow at midday.'

EGYPTIAN MAIL

WHO ARE ALL THESE PEOPLE?
THE USUAL SUSPECTS...

We sat on the terrace in the afternoon sun. Mr Fish told me about his life as a diamond dealer in Amsterdam.

'By 1937, I could see what was coming so I shifted operations,' he said.

Filing invoices and making the morning tea at Brown and Dureau couldn't have felt any further away.

He asked me about Evans Bay. He asked me about Takoradi and Kwame. He ordered more beer, then handed me an envelope of cash and explained how many ingots it would buy.

'Just a few to start with,' he said.

'How do you know I'll be back?'

'I know where to find you.'

The next week we were on our way back down the Nile. We weren't squeezed in the Blenheim. We were in the huge comfy seats of an Imperial Airways flying boat. The same aircraft that Ben and I had seen from the fourteen footer in Evans Bay. There were five-course meals with five-star service, fold-down beds and a stand-up bar, and I had Mr Fish's envelope of cash in my top pocket.

Back in Takoradi I went to see Kwame.

'And how would you get the gold on the plane?' he asked. 'And then get it off at the other end? There are ground crew and mechanics and officers and military police with big sticks standing at the gate. You'll end up being court-martialled, doing time in a military prison, then flying a desk in El Fasher for the rest of the war. Gold will get you into trouble, Mr Witcombe.'

'If Kwame's not in, it won't work,' said Arky at breakfast, 'and having long conversations with Leo in the squalid heat of El Fasher doesn't appeal to me in the slightest.'

Perhaps Kwame was right. We'd never get the gold past the military police at the gate in Takoradi. But Mr Fish did tell me there were no military police in Kano.

'What do you need this ammo box for?' said the harried aircraftsman preparing us for take-off at Kano.

'Don't want to bump into those Vichy French,' said Dudunski.

'I thought they'd gone over to de Gaulle,' said the aircraftsman as he helped stash the box on board.

'Best to play it safe,' said Dudunski.

'Just this once,' muttered Arky, as he settled into the pilot's seat.

When we stepped out onto the tarmac at Abu Sueir air base outside Cairo, the rubbish collection cart came by, just like Mr Fish said it would.

'You're not supposed to be out here!' yelled the ground crew. 'Get your smelly cart off the runway!'

The ammo box full of gold ingots was slipped under the grubby tarpaulin covering the rubbish. The donkey cart ambled off. It rolled out of the main gate, merged into the honking traffic and plodded all the way into the city — to the Kahn El Kalili Bazaar where Mr Fish was waiting.

The forty thousand thieves

Cairo, January, 1942

The next morning I met Mr Fish on the terrace at Shepherds Hotel.

'An excellent load of rubbish,' he said.

'What happens to the gold now?' I asked.

He waved his arm around the terrace.

'Some is bought by dealers who trade it for guns. Some goes to those Americans over there who fly it back across the Atlantic. Some is made into jewellery and the Germans are always short of gold reserves.'

'You mean we're helping fund the German war effort?'

'Money doesn't have morals, Mr Witcombe.'

'I don't want to know any more.'

Mr Fish reached into his jacket pocket, took out an envelope and handed it to me.

'Here's your payment plus funding for the next run.' I looked in the envelope.

'There's a lot of notes in here.'

'It's all correct, as we agreed,' said Mr Fish. He looked at his watch, said he had another meeting, and hurried off down the steps. Now I could afford to order a beer. At the next table was a Kiwi officer drawing on a large pad.

'Can I buy you a drink?' I asked.

'That would be grand,' said the officer, looking up from his drawing.

'Name's Peter,' he said. 'War artist.'

'The army pays you to draw pictures?'

'They do.'

'Can I look?'

'Sure,' he said, turning the pad around. There was a drawing of a general.

'That's General Freyberg!'

'Good, I must have nailed him. Mostly I paint portraits of the top brass. It's hard to get them to relax and look human. I prefer drawing Freyberg's forty thousand thieves in the desert. They don't pose. They just

carry on playing two up and firing up the Benghazi burner for a brew. You have to be quick on the draw. What about you?'

'I'm just one of the forty thousand thieves.'

'Let's get you down on paper then,' he said. He looked intently at me, then down at the paper, the pencil moving in big, rapid strokes. He stopped, looked up at me, then back down at the drawing. There was another flurry with the pencil, then he held it out at arm's length, added a few more strokes and declared it to be OK. It looked more than OK to me. It was magic.

'Let me buy you another beer,' I said.

Peter carefully tore the page out of the pad and handed it to me.

'A fair swap,' he said.

I counted the cash into three equal shares. My share was more than I earned in a year at Brown and Dureau! No more barracks; or breakfast, dinner and a cut lunch from a widow in Newtown. We set ourselves up in a hotel on Gezira Island while we waited for transport back to Takoradi.

The hotel was run by Aziz. He manned the front desk. He operated the lift and served breakfast. The island was quieter than central Cairo. We were on the second floor, the dining room opened on to a leafy green balcony. There were sliced tomatoes, cucumbers and flatbread for breakfast with tahini and figs and hard-boiled eggs and strong coffee that Aziz brewed in a small metal jug.

Aziz sat us with Mrs Nikolayeva for breakfast. 'You will like Mrs Nikolayeva,' he said. It was more an instruction than an opinion. Mrs Nikolayeva was in a wheelchair and she lived in the hotel. She scolded Arky and Dudunski for sticking to tea, toast and marmalade. Before the war she had worked at the Hermitage in Leningrad.

'Why is there a hermitage in the middle of Leningrad?' I asked.

'It's an art gallery, you dolt,' growled Mrs Nikolayeva. 'The biggest art gallery in the world. I was a gilder.'

'A what?'

'A gilder. I put gold leaf on the frames of the paintings. We had the best. The best of the French painters.' Her voice became soft and gentle when she talked about the paintings. 'When they started selling paintings to fund the five-year plans, I knew it was time to leave. I crossed the Black Sea from Odessa to Istanbul on a rusting steamer — the captain was very accommodating. From Istanbul I made my way to Cairo where I worked in the Egyptian Museum. Have you been?' she demanded.

'Yes, yes,' I said. 'So much to see.'

'Here they know all about gold,' said Mrs Nikolayeva. 'The flesh of the gods, the pharaohs called it. And what about you boys?' she asked. 'What brings you here?'

'Gold,' said Dudunski.

At night we'd have dinner at Groppi's and then head off to the Kit Kat Club or a party on the houseboats at the end of the island.

On our next flight out of Kano there were three heavy ammo boxes in the back of the Blenheim. For a modest payment, the lads on the ground at Kano lost interest in what was in the ammo boxes.

One hour out of El Geneina, Arky peered at the horizon. 'I don't like the look of those clouds,' he said. A giant wall of brown, like smoke from a giant bush fire was rolling towards us.

'Those aren't clouds, that's a sandstorm,' I said. 'We can't fly through that; we'll suck sand into the engines.'

We'd been told about the violent winds in the middle of sandstorms.

'I'm not flying into that to find El Fasher,' said Arky. 'We'll just have to stay up here, flying around in circles.'

We did just that, watching as the fuel gauge ticked towards empty.

Slowly, the desert appeared again, trails of sand behind the storm fading away. It was a relief to see Leo padding down the veranda to greet us.

We didn't need the donkey and the rubbish cart at Abu Sueir now. For another payment, the ground crew had arranged a delivery truck.

The next day I met Mr Fish on the terrace at Shepherds. He handed over another large envelope of cash.

'It's all there, as we agreed.'

After two more trips, I didn't know where to stash all the cash. I had pockets full of notes, there were notes under the mattress, cash in the drawer of the bedside table. I was losing track of it all. I put it all in my kitbag and walked over the river to the National Bank of Egypt.

'Servicemen like you don't need bank accounts,' said the teller. 'You're only paid enough to live from week to week.'

'I know, we're like the penny divers,' I said.

The teller looked puzzled.

'Never mind,' I said by way of explanation and placed the kitbag on the counter. The teller looked inside.

'I see,' he said. 'There are forms to fill in.'

Back in Takoradi there was a line of new American DC3s out on the runway.

I called into Stores to catch up with Kwame. He was up a ladder stacking American uniforms on the shelves.

'It's getting busy,' he said. 'The Americans are flying planes across the South Atlantic from Brazil now. Pass me up some of those boxes, will you?' I grabbed a couple of boxes and passed them up.

'And how's the gold business going?' he asked.

'How do you know about that?'

There are very few secrets here, Mr Witcombe.'

'It's nothing to be ashamed of,' I said. 'We're in Transport Command, we're traders, we move things from place to place, that's all.'

'Just like the slave ships,' said Kwame, as he climbed down the ladder. 'Be careful, Mr Witcombe. King Farouk runs the gold business in Cairo. He does not take kindly to competitors.'

IF YOU CAME TO WORK FOR US THERE WOULD BE NO TROUBLE.

WHO IS 'US'?

THAT DOESN'T MATTER.

TALK TO MR DUDUNSKI AND MR ARKWRIGHT ABOUT OUR PROPOSAL.

Tea?' asked Aziz as we sat down for breakfast the next morning.

'Yes please,' said Mrs Nikolayeva.

'It's getting a bit dicey,' I said, reaching for the tahini. I described my encounter on the bridge.

Arky stirred his tea. Dudunski buttered his toast.

'This started as a lark on the side,' said Dudunski.

'A lucrative lark,' said Arky.

'It was OK when it was one ammo box in the back of the Blenheim,' said Dudunski. 'It's too big now — we're turning into crooks.'

'We're not crooks, we're couriers,' said Arky. 'The boys on the bridge need us, we've got the aeroplanes. We can negotiate.'

'I'm wondering if "negotiating" might mean "do it our way or end up face down in the mud under the bridge."' I said.

'Look,' said Arky. 'Rommel's on the run. We'll be moved on soon. Until we're shipped out, we stick together.'

'We can't trust anyone,' said Dudunski. 'The guy with the rubbish cart at Abu Sueir, the one we replaced with a truck, who will he be talking to?'

'More tea?' asked Aziz.

'Yes please,' said Mrs Nikolayeva.

The last leg of the Benghazi handicap

Cairo, June 1943

The Benghazi handicap had raced back and forth across the top of Africa since 1940. First the Italians attacked the Brits. The Brits pushed them back. Then the Germans reinforced the Italians and pushed the British back to the little railway halt at El Alamein. Whoever had the most tanks, petrol and aeroplanes would win that leg of the war.

Around and around we flew. Takoradi, Cairo. Cairo, Takoradi. We knew the jungle and desert now, we knew the seasons for sandstorms. The stops on the way were better supplied; Leo would meet each new group of fliers at El Fasher. We lost three more planes but that was due to mechanical failure, not an error of navigation.

Come 1943, we had delivered thousands of planes across the desert. Enough to defeat Rommel at El Alamein and chase him back along the top of Africa. The Americans had landed in Morocco — Rommel was being squeezed from both ends. By the middle of 1943, what was left of his army surrendered in Tunisia.

Whenever there was space on a flight back to England, now it was filled with pilots, navigators, gunners and mechanics who had finished their tour of duty and were on their way home or were being re-assigned to Italy or the Pacific.

Arky and Dudunski got the first flight. They had two days' notice. We thought about going to the Kit Kat Club one last time, but decided it was probably best to stay out of sight and instead spent an evening yarning on the balcony.

'I'm going to miss my boys,' said Mrs Nikolayeva.

A week after they left, I received my marching orders.

On Thursday morning, there was a loud knock on my hotel room door. Two large Military Policemen stood there. They had red caps, white holsters and black armbands with the letters M P on them. They strode into the room and looked around. They checked in the wardrobe, they looked under the bed. One of them studied Peter's drawing that I had pinned to the wall, while the other opened the drawer of the bedside table and pulled out my bankbook.

I remembered Mr Fish's description: British spies spying on German agents spying on Americans spying on French arms dealers. It hadn't occurred to me that someone would be spying on Mr Fish.

I looked at the mean-looking Webley revolvers in their bright white holsters and wondered who they were working for. The Brits? King Farouk? Themselves? They turned, and marched out the door.

'Close that account,' they said again and strode down the hotel corridor to the lift.

I knew what an investigation would mean, a court martial, a long spell in a military prison and all the cash in my account would disappear. That cash was coming with me back home to Wellington. There was enough to buy a nice car and my own house with a full drinks cabinet. I was never going back to Brown and Dureau. Ever.

I pulled back the curtain. A swirl of black crows wheeled across the early morning sky. I grabbed the bankbook off the bedside table, fished my kitbag out of the wardrobe and pulled the door shut behind me.

'Coffee?' enquired Aziz as I hurried through the dining room.

'Not this morning.'

I clanged shut the lattice door of the ancient lift, creaked my way to the ground floor and legged it down the street towards the river. The morning heat was tempered by a cool breeze off the Nile. The National Bank was opening its doors when I arrived.

'All of it?' asked the teller.

'Yes, all of it. Stuff it in here.' I pushed the kitbag across the counter.

Clutching the kitbag to my chest I caught a taxi to the Khan El-Khalili Bazar and found Charlie Fish.

He opened the kitbag and looked in. He showed no surprise.

'Back to New Zealand?'

'All the way home,' I said.

'I can do diamonds and Thomas Cook travellers cheques.'

I didn't know what a traveller's cheque was. Mr Fish had to explain. 'You sign them twice. Once when you buy the cheque and then you sign it again when you want to turn it back into cash. They're perfectly legal. You have to have the money up front to buy them, but that's no problem for you, Mr Witcombe. The Thomas Cook agency is right next door to Shepherds. Diamonds, well, they're small and easy to hide and I can do a deal for you right now. If you lose the cheques you'll still have the diamonds and if you lose the diamonds you'll still have the cheques.'

Back in my room I unpicked Win's stitching along the hem of my coat, put in the diamonds and sewed it up again. I stuffed all the traveller's cheques in the kitbag, laid some clothes over the top and went to find Aziz.

'I'm flying out tomorrow, Aziz. I need you to keep this safe for me until I leave.'

Aziz took the kitbag and looked at the fistful of notes I gave him. 'That's very generous, Mr Witcombe.'

'I liked your coffee, Aziz.'

Early on Friday morning there was another knock at the bedroom door. It was the two military policeman. They were carrying big wooden truncheons.

'We've come for your kitbag,' they said.

'I don't have a kitbag.'

'Don't muck us about, Mr Witcombe. The kitbag you left the bank with.'

They pushed me aside and barged into the room. They ripped the sheets off the bed, flipped over the mattress. Yanked the wardrobe away from the wall.

'Where is it?' they demanded, one jabbing me in the guts with his truncheon. The other took a swing at my head.

I ducked and shoved over the wardrobe. It knocked them both to the floor. I shot out the door, locked it behind me and bounded down the corridor to the dining room.

'Quick, in the kitchen,' said Aziz. He slammed the door of the lift shut and sent it clanking to the ground floor. Mrs Nikolayeva whizzed her wheelchair across the room and parked herself in front of the kitchen door. There was the sound of a shot down the corridor and the door being kicked open. The MPs burst into the dining room waving their revolvers. Mrs Nikolayeva pointed at the lift. The two MPs thundered down the stairs and out onto the street.

I opened the kitchen door and peeked out.

'More fun than the Kit Kat Club,' said Mrs Nikolayeva.

We waited for twenty minutes.

'I'll check if the coast is clear,' said Mrs Nikolayeva. 'If it is, I'll grab you a cab.' She took the lift to the street and wheeled her way up and down the

pavement. There was no sign of the redcaps. Aziz watched from the balcony. Mrs Nikolayeva gave a thumbs up from the opposite side of the street.

Aziz grabbed my kitbag out of the dirty laundry basket where he'd been keeping it. 'Good luck,' he said.

A DC3 was waiting out on the tarmac. 'There's an hour before we leave,' said one of the American pilots. 'Come and have coffee with us.'

Half an hour before boarding, the two military policemen arrived and stood at the bottom of the boarding stairs.

Damn, I thought. They must have seen my name on the list.

The last to board were a couple with a baby bundled up in blankets.

'I need to look through those blankets,' said the MP.

'I've just got him to sleep,' said the woman. She reached into her bag and pulled out a nappy, 'If you're going to wake him up you can change him too.'

The redcaps waved them up the stairs and turned to the waiting aircrew.

'What's in these sacks?' they asked.

'They're US mail bags,' said the pilot. 'Did you find what you were looking for?'

'Not here.'

'We'll be off then.'

The three air crew heaved the mail sacks on board, climbed in, slammed the door shut and walked up the sloping aisle towards the cockpit.

'Dumb spooks must think it's called a DC3 because it takes three to fly it,' said the pilot.

I took off my aviator sunglasses, my American air force cap and my American flight jacket and gave them back to the pilot. I untied the top of one of the US mail sacks. Underneath the mail I found my kitbag and my RAF greatcoat. I buckled myself in next to the couple with the baby for the long journey back to cold, damp England.

Press button B to get your money back

Wellington, 1944

The waitress thrust the coat at me. I felt the tiny hard diamonds in the hem and gave her twenty bucks.

'Jeez mister, that's more than the coat's worth.'

I sailed from San Francisco on a passenger liner in wartime battle dress of drab grey. It was jammed with returning Kiwis. The food was great. The weather was fine. The ship was faster than any prowling submarine. We lay in the sun on deck and told stories about the desert war. Every time I told the story of the Takoradi Run, the sandstorms and the parties in Cairo grew bigger. I didn't mention my mates that had crashed in the desert and I left out the diamonds and the kitbag full of traveller's cheques.

The weather became cooler. The ship sailed into Cook Strait. I could see Island Bay where Win and I went on the tram with our mum and had Frosty Jack ice creams. What would Mum think if she had lived? I guess she'd approve of the P class and the fourteen-footer and maybe she'd even approve of me joining the Air Force, but the gold smuggling and kitbag full of cash? Maybe not. Did I feel guilty? I really wasn't sure.

I could see now that her death had destroyed the old man. His marriage to Anne Duncan was a marriage of convenience, perhaps even companionship — I found out later that Anne Duncan's first husband had died in the flu epidemic — but I didn't understand that when I got the job at Brown and Dureau and shot through.

The ship turned into Wellington Harbour. Ward Island looked just like it had when Ben and I made our first run in our P class dinghies and camped there overnight. I could see down the long reach of Evans Bay

where the flying boats from Australia had landed. We rounded Point Jerningham into the inner harbour where Ben and I raced the fourteen footer. There was the city, a little shabbier, but much as we left it.

We said goodbye to our shipboard mates.

'Here's my address.'

'Yes, I'll write.'

'Have you got my phone number?'

'Keep in touch.'

I wasn't good at keeping in touch. Telephones, letters — that wasn't me. I never did send Win the necklace I bought in Takoradi.

'I know you won't get around to writing,' Ben had said. 'But that's OK, we'll catch up sooner or later.' Tomorrow I'd go to his house on the hill with all those books and the garage. I'd find out where he was. Tomorrow I'd go to the Thomas Cook agency — was it still on James Smith corner? — and sign those traveller's cheques. Then I'd go to the big jewellery shop on the corner of Willis St with the diamonds. Mr Fish had told me the price.

'They'll start much lower,' he'd said. 'Just wait them out.'

'Won't they want to know where I got the diamonds?'

'Money doesn't have morals, Mr Witcombe.'

I wondered if I did? I heard Kwame's voice. 'Gold will get you into trouble.' Maybe it still would.

I knew how to navigate my way to Berlin in the dark and how to avoid sandstorms in the Sahara. Not the best qualifications for a peace-time job.

A tug nudged the ship into Pipitea Wharf. Wives waved. There were mothers in tears and awkward hugs with children wondering who the strange man from the big ship was.

I hadn't let Dad, Win or Anne Duncan know that I was on the boat. The crowds left. The wounded were carried off. I walked away through the empty city.

There was a red phone box on a corner. I stopped. I could remember the number. I pushed open the door and put pennies in the slot.

Win answered.

You pressed button A to connect or button B to get your money back.

I pressed button A.

...IS THAT YOU, RON?

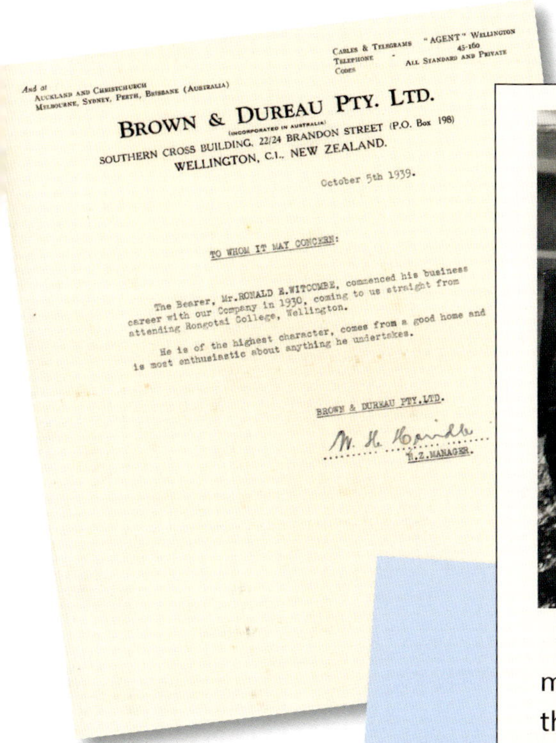

Cables & Telegrams "AGENT" Wellington
Telephone - 45-160
Codes All Standard and Private

And at
Auckland and Christchurch
Melbourne, Sydney, Perth, Brisbane (Australia)

BROWN & DUREAU PTY. LTD.
(INCORPORATED IN AUSTRALIA)
SOUTHERN CROSS BUILDING, 22/24 BRANDON STREET (P.O. Box 198)
WELLINGTON, C.1., NEW ZEALAND.

October 5th 1939.

TO WHOM IT MAY CONCERN:

The Bearer, Mr. RONALD E. WITCOMBE, commenced his business career with our Company in 1930, coming to us straight from attending Rongotai College, Wellington.

He is of the highest character, comes from a good home and is most enthusiastic about anything he undertakes.

BROWN & DUREAU PTY. LTD.

N.Z. MANAGER.

Ron Witcombe was born in 1915. He joined the New Zealand Air Force in 1939.

Ron was never mentioned around the dinner table. He was far too colourful for our buttoned-down Presbyterian family where the most important thing was to be proper.

Ron wasn't always proper. He was a lad on the make. When I met him towards the end of his life, the story of his war years came tumbling out. To join up his story I had to imagine some things. I created his two buddies, Arky and Dudunski, and I went to Takoradi and Cairo to get a sense of what he may have experienced.

I hope he would approve of this occasionally imaginative telling of his story.

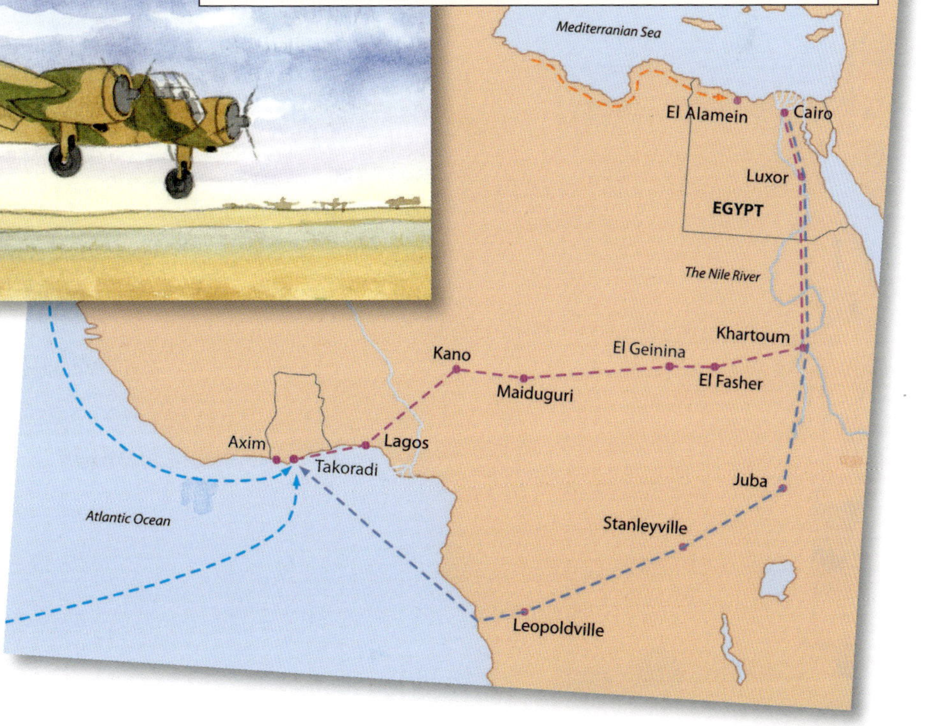

Published in 2026 by David Bateman Ltd
2/5 Workspace Drive
Hobsonville, Auckland 0618
New Zealand

www.batemanbooks.co.nz

ISBN 978-1-77689-154-2

Illustrations: Bob Kerr

Photographs from the collection of Bob Kerr.

Map of Cairo on page 45 from the Auckland Libraries Heritage Collections, Map 36540A.

Book design: Bob Kerr and Adrian Kinnaird.

Printed in China by Asia Pacific Offset Ltd